Sarah Hatton Knits 10 Crochet Projects
WITH HELPFUL TECHNIQUES

First published in Great Britain in 2014 by
Quail Publishing
www.quailpublishing.co.uk

Designs: Sarah Hatton
Photography: India Hobson
Styling: Sarah Hatton
Model: Kristie at Boss Models
Flowers: Emma at orchisfloraldesign.com
Graphic Design: Darren Brant

ISBN 978-0-9567851-6-9

Printed in the United Kingdom

SARAH HATTON KNITS

10 SIMPLE

CROCHET PROJECTS

WITH HELPFUL TECHNIQUES

Q
QUAIL

Introduction

Welcome to the the fourth book in the sarah hatton knits cosy series, however this issue is something of a departure as it is an introduction to crochet.

Crochet is set to be a big trend on the catwalk this summer so this book is designed to help take your first steps into the techniques. We have forgone the complication abbreviations that can sometimes seem like another language and can seem very daunting.

The book features simple scarves and hats which are quick to work through to more substantially projects such as the cardigan or shrug.

We are hoping this book helps you feel as excited as we do about a summer of crochet!

CAPE/PONCHO

PAGE. 16

Worked in Rowan All Seasons Cotton

EYELET CARDIGAN

PAGE. 19

Worked in Rowan All Seasons Cotton

EYELET HAT

PAGE. 23

Worked in Rowan All Seasons Cotton

STRIPED HAT

PAGE. 25

Worked in Rowan Softknit Cotton

BUCKET BAG

PAGE. 28

Worked in Rowan All Seasons Chunky

SHRUG

PAGE. 30

Worked in Rowan Softknit Cotton

Chevron Scarf

Page. 34

Worked in Rowan Softknit Cotton

STRIPED SCARF

PAGE. 36

Worked in Rowan Handknit Cotton

Collar

Page. 38

Worked in Rowan Softknit Cotton

MESH COWL
PAGE. 40

Worked in Rowan All Seasons Chunky

CAPE/PONCHO

ROWAN ALL SEASONS COTTON

FINISHED SIZE

	S	M	L	
Approx width (laid flat)	54	65	78	cm
	21½	25½	30½	in
Length	37	38	39	cm
	14½	15	15½	in

MATERIALS

YARN
Rowan All Seasons Cotton 5 [6:7] x 50gm
Shown in Cardboard 243

HOOK
5mm (US H8) crochet hook

TENSION
13 stitches and 8 rows measures 10cm/4in
over treble pattern using 5mm (US H8)
crochet hook.

Make 59[71:72] chains loosely, join with a
slip stitch into the 1st chain to form a ring.

Round 1: Chain 3 (counts as 1st treble),
1 treble into each stitch to end, slip stitch
into 3rd chain at beginning of round.
59 [71:72] stitches.

Repeat this round 7 [7:5] times more.

For L size only
Next round: Chain 3 (counts as 1st
treble),* 2 treble into next stitch, 1 treble
into next 4 stitches, repeat from * to last
stitch, 1 treble into last stitch, slip stitch
into 3rd chain at beginning of round.
[86] stitches.

Work 1 round as given for round 1.

For all sizes
Next round: Chain 3 (counts as 1st
treble), 1 treble into next stitch, * 2 treble
into next stitch, 1 treble into next 2
stitches, repeat from * to end, slip stitch
into 3rd chain at beginning of round.
78 [94:114] stitches.

Work 2 rounds as given for round 1.

Next round: Chain 3 (counts as 1st
treble), 1 treble into next stitch, * 2 treble
into next stitch, 1 treble into next 3
stitches, repeat from * to end, slip stitch
into 3rd chain at beginning of round.
97 [117:142] stitches.

Work 2 rounds as given for round 1.

Next round: Chain 3 (counts as 1st
treble), 1 treble into next stitch, * 2 treble
into next stitch, 1 treble into next 4
stitches, repeat from * to end, slip stitch
into 3rd chain at beginning of round.
116 [140:170] stitches.

Work 1 round as given for round 1.

Next round: Chain 3 (counts as 1st
treble), 1 treble into next   stitch, * 2 treble
into next stitch, 1 treble into next 5
stitches, repeat from * to end, slip stitch
into 3rd chain at beginning of round.

135 [163:198] stitches.

Work 1 [2:3] rounds as given for round 1.

Scallop edge
Round 1: Chain 6 (counts as 1st treble and 3 chain), work 1 treble into same place, * chain 2, miss next 6 stitches, (1 treble, 3 chain, 1 treble) into next stitch, repeat from * to last 6 stitches, chain 2, miss next 6 stitches, slip stitch to 3rd chain at beginning of round.

Round 2: Chain 3 (counts as 1st treble), work 7 trebles into next 3 chain space, * work 8 trebles into next 3 chain space, repeat from * to end, slip stitch to 3rd chain at beginning of round.

Round 3: Slip stitch across to 4th treble of 1st group of trebles, chain 6 (counts as 1st treble and 3 chain), work 1 treble into next stitch, * chain 3, miss next 6 stitches, 1 treble into next stitch, 3 chain, 1 treble into next stitch, repeat from * to last 6 stitches, chain 3, miss next 6 stitches, slip stitch to 3rd chain at beginning of round.

Repeat the last two rounds twice, then round 1 of scallop edge once more.

Cut yarn and fasten off. Sew in ends.

EYELET CARDIGAN

ROWAN ALL SEASONS COTTON

FINISHED SIZE

S	M	L	XL	XXL	
To fit bust					
81-86	91-96	102-107	112-117	122-127	cm
32-34	36-38	40-42	44-46	48-50	in
Actual width					
46	51	57	63	70	cm
(Laid flat)					
18	20	22½	25	27½	in
Length					
54	56	58	60	62	cm
21½	22	23	23¾	24½	in
Sleeve length					
29	30	30	31	31	cm
11½	12	12	12¼	12¼	in

MATERIALS

YARN
9 [10:11:13:14] x 50gm
Rowan All Seasons Cotton
Shown in Denim 249

HOOK
5mm (H8) crochet hook

TENSION
13 stitches and 8 rows measures 10cm/4in
over treble pattern using 5mm (UK H8)
crochet hook.

BODY
Make 124 [138:150:168:186] chains.
Row 1: Work 1 treble into 4ᵗʰ chain from
hook, work 1 treble into each stitch to
end, turn.
121 [135:147:165:183] stitches.

Row 2: Chain 3, miss 1 treble, 1 treble
into each stitch to end, work 1 treble into
3ʳᵈ of chain at beginning of last row, turn.

Row 3: Chain 3, miss 1 treble, * 1 treble
into next stitch, chain 1, miss 1 stitch,
repeat from * to last 2 stitches, 1 treble
into each stitch to end, working last st into
turning chain. Turn.

Repeat these 2 rows once.

Row 6: As row 2.

Rows 7 to 10: As rows 2 and 3 twice.

Now working in treble fabric (just
repeating row 2) throughout continue
as follows:-

Continue until work measures

34[35:36:37:38]cm/
13½ [13¾:14:14½:15]in.

Shape armholes
Row 1: Chain 3, miss 1 treble, 1 treble into next 27 [31:31:36:41] stitches, turn and continue on these stitches only for front.

Row 2: Chain 3, miss 1 treble, 1 treble into each stitch to end, work 1 treble into 3rd of chain at beginning of last row, turn.

Repeat row 2 until work measures 20 [21:22:23:24]cm/8 [8¼:8¾:9:9½]in from start of armhole.

Cut yarn and fasten off.

(You may wish to keep a note of how many rows you work to make sure the rest of your garment matches)

Continuing on Row 1 of armhole shaping, work as follows:-

Row 1: Miss 4 [4:8:8:8] stitches, chain 3, miss 1 treble, 1 treble into next 60 [66:72:80:88] stitches, turn and continue on these stitches only for back.

Row 2: Chain 3, miss 1 treble, 1 treble into each stitch to end, work 1 treble into 3rd of chain at beginning of last row, turn.

Repeat row 2 until work matches front armhole.

Cut yarn and fasten off.

Again continuing along row 1 of armhole shaping, work as follows:-

Row 1: Miss 4 [4:8:8:8] stitches, chain 3, miss 1 treble, 1 treble into next 27 [31:31:36:41] stitches, turn and continue on these stitches only for front.

Row 2: Chain 3, miss 1 treble, 1 treble into each stitch to end, work 1 treble into 3rd of chain at beginning of last row, turn.

Repeat row 2 until work matches first front and back armhole.

Cut yarn and fasten off.

SLEEVES (Both alike)

Make 38 [40:42:44:46] chains.
Row 1: Work 1 treble into 4th chain from hook, work 1 treble into each stitch to end, turn. 35 [37:39:41:43] stitches.

Row 2: Chain 3, miss 1 treble, 1 treble into each stitch to end, work 1 treble into 3rd of chain at beginning of last row.

Row 3: Chain 3, miss 1 treble, * 1 treble into next stitch, chain 1, miss 1 stitch, repeat from * to last 2 stitches, 1 treble into each stitch, turn.

Row 4 (increase row): Chain 3, work 1 treble into first stitch, 1 treble into each stitch until 1 stitch remains, work 2 treble into next stitch, work 1 treble into 3rd of chain at beginning of last row, turn. 37 [39:41:43:45] stitches.

Row 5: As row 3.

Row 6: As row 2.

Row 7: As row 3.

Row 8: As row 4.

Next row: Chain 3, miss 1 treble, 1 treble into each stitch to end, work 1 treble into 3rd of chain at beginning of last row, turn.

This row sets treble fabric.

Working in treble fabric throughout, increase 1 stitch at each end (as set in row 4) of next and 2 [2:3:3:3] following 5th [5th:4th:4th:4th] rows. 45 [47:51:53:55] stitches.

Cont without shaping until sleeve measures approx. 29 [30:30:31:31] cm/11½[12:12:12¼:12¼]in, place marker to show end of sleeve, then work 1 [1:2:2:2] rows more which will then be sewn in place to gaps left at armholes in body.

Shape sleeve top

Next row: Slip stitch across to 6th treble, make 3 chain, miss 1st stitch, work 1 treble into each stitch to last 5 stitches.

Repeat this row 3 times more.

Cut yarn and fasten off.

MAKING UP

Either using a crochet slip stitch through both pieces of fabric or by sewing the seam, join sleeve seams to markers. Leaving 18 [18:19:19:20:20]cm/7 [7:7½:7½:8:8]in open at centre to form neck, join shoulder seams.

Placing the section at the top of the sleeve from the marker to the end along the gap left in the body, sew the sleeves in position.

FINISHED SIZE
55 [60]cm/21½ [23½]in

MATERIALS

YARN
Rowan All Seasons Cotton
2 x 50gm
Shown in Denim 249

HOOK
5mm (US H8) crochet hook

TENSION
13 stitches and 8 rows measures
10cm/4in using a 5mm (US H8) crochet
hook

Make 72 [78] chains loosely, join with a
slip stitch into the 1st chain to form a ring.

Round 1: Make 1 chain, work 1 double
crochet into each chain to the end, slip
stitch to chain at beginning of round to
join. 71 stitches.

Rep this round 4 times more.

Round 5: Make 3 chains (this counts as
the first treble), work 1 treble into each
stitch to end to round, slip stitch to 3rd
chain at beginning of round to join.

Round 6: Make 5 chains (counts as
1 treble and 2 chains) miss 2 stitches, *
work 1 treble into next stitch, work 2
chain, miss 2 stitches, repeat from * to
last 3 sts, work 1 treble into next stitch,
work 2 chain, miss 2 stitches, slip stitch to
3rd chain at beginning of round to join.

Round 7: Make 3 chains, * work
2 trebles into next chain space, work
1 treble into next stitch, rep from * to last
3 sts, work 1 treble into next stitch, work
2 trebles into next chain space, slip stitch
to 3rd chain at beginning of round to join.

EYELET HAT
ROWAN ALL SEASONS COTTON

Repeat these 2 rounds twice more.

Round 11: Make 3 chains (this counts as the first treble), work 1 treble into each stitch to end to round, slip stitch to 3rd chain at beginning of round to join.

Repeat this round until work measures 17cm/6$^{1}/_{2}$in.

Shape crown

Next round: Make 3 chains, * treble 2 together (by taking yarn round hook, place hook into next stitch and draw through yarn, take yarn back over hook and draw through the first 2 loops on the hook, take yarn back over needle and place hook into next stitch, take yarn over hook and draw through yarn, take yarn back over hook and draw through first 2 loops on the hook, take yarn back over hook and pull through all three loops on the hook), 1 treble into next 4 stitches, repeat from * to last 5 stitches, treble 2 together, treble into next 3 stitches, slip stitch to 3rd chain at beginning of round to join. 60 [65] stitches.

Next 2 rounds: As round 11.
Next round: Make 3 chains, * treble 2 together , 1 treble into next 3 stitches, repeat from * to last 4 stitches, treble 2 together, treble into next 2 stitches, slip stitch to 3rd chain at beginning of round to join. 48 [52] stitches.

Next round: Make 3 chains, * treble 2 together , 1 treble into next 2 stitches, repeat from * to last 3 stitches, treble 2 together, treble into next stitch, slip stitch to 3rd chain at beginning of round to join. 36 [39] stitches.

Next round: Make 3 chains, * treble 2 together , 1 treble into next stitch, repeat from * to last 2 stitches, treble 2 together, slip stitch to 3rd chain at beginning of round to join. 24 [26] stitches.

Next round: 1 chain, 1 double crochet into each stitch, slip stitch to chain at beginning of round to join.

Next round: 1 chain, * double crochet 2 together (place hook into next stitch and take yarn over hook, draw yarn through work, place hook into next stitch and take yarn over hook and draw yarn through work, take yarn over hook and pull through all 3 loops on hook), repeat from * to end, slip stitch to first stitch. 12 [13] stitches.

Break yarn and fasten off, thread through remaining stitches and pull up tight before securing.

Striped Hat

Rowan Softknit Cotton

FINISHED SIZE
56 [60]cm/ 22[23½]in

MATERIALS

YARN
Rowan Softknit Cotton
A – Dark Lime 579 1 x 50gm
B – Seaweed 581 2 x 50gm

Also suitable for Rowan Handknit Cotton

HOOK
4mm (G6) crochet hook

TENSION
15 stitches and 10 rows measures
10cm/4in using a 4mm (G6) crochet
hook.

USEFUL INFORMATION
To change colour, insert hook into top of
3ch, draw through new colour instead of
old. Continue with next round.

Using yarn A, make 84 [90] chains loosely,
join with a slip stitch into the 1st chain to
form a ring.

Round 1: Make 1 chain, work 1 double
crochet into each chain to the end, slip
stitch to chain at beginning of round to
join.

Rep this round 3 times more, changing to
yarn B on the last slip stich.

Round 5: Using yarn B, make 3 chains
(this counts as the first treble), miss stitch
at base of chain, work 1 treble into each
stitch to end of round, slip stitch to 3rd
chain at beginning of round to join.

Round 6: Work as round 5, changing to
yarn A on the last slip stitch.

Rounds 7 and 8: Using yarn A, work
as row 5, changing to yarn B on last slip
stitch.

Working in yarn B throughout, work
as set on round 5 until work measures
17cm/6½in.

Shape crown
Next round: Make 3 chains, * treble 2
together (by taking yarn round hook, place
hook into next stitch and draw through
yarn, 3 loops on hook, take yarn back over
hook and draw through the first 2 loops
on the hook, take yarn back over needle
and place hook into next stitch, take yarn
over hook and draw through yarn, take
yarn back over hook and draw through
first 2 loops on the hook, take yarn back
over hook and pull through all three loops
on the hook), 1 treble into next 4 stitches,
repeat from * to last 5 stitches, treble 2
together, treble into next 3 stitches, slip
stitch to 3rd chain at beginning of round to
join. 70 [75] stitches.

Next round: As round 5.

Next round: Make 3 chains, miss stitch
at base of chain, * treble 2 together , 1
treble into next 3 stitches, repeat from * to
last 4 stitches, treble 2 together, treble into
next 2 stitches, slip stitch to 3rd chain at beginning of round to join. 56 [60] stitches.

Next round: As round 5.

Next round: Make 3 chains, miss stitch
at base of chain, * treble 2 together , 1
treble into next 2 stitches, repeat from * to
last 3 stitches, treble 2 together, treble into
next stitch, slip stitch to 3rd chain at beginning of round to join. 42 [45] stitches.

Next round: Make 3 chains, miss stitch

at base of chain, * treble 2 together , 1
treble into next stitch, repeat from * to last
2 stitches, treble 2 together, slip stitch to 3rd
chain at beginning of round to join.
28 [30] stitches.

Next round: Make 3 chains, miss stitch
at base of chain, * treble 2 together, repeat
from * to last stitch, 1 treble into next stitch.
slip stitch to 3rd chain at beginning of round
to join. 15 [16] stitches.

Next round: 1 chain, 1 double crochet
into each stitch, slip stitch to chain at beginning of round to join.

Next round: 1 chain, * double crochet 2
together (place hook into next stitch and
take yarn over hook, draw yarn through
work, place hook into next stitch and take
yarn over hook and draw yarn through
work, take yarn over hook and pull through
all 3 loops on hook), repeat from * to last 1
[0] stitches, work 1 [0] double crochet into
next stitch, slip stitch to first stitch.
8 stitches.

Break yarn and fasten off, thread through
remaining stitches and pull up tight before
securing.

BUCKET BAG

ROWAN ALL SEASONS COTTON CHUNKY

FINISHED SIZE (APPROX.)
42cm/16½in wide x 40cm/15½in deep (laid flat)

MATERIALS

YARN
All Seasons Cotton Chunky
4 x 100gm
Shown in Stoney 610

HOOK
8mm (US L) crochet hook

TENSION
8 stitches and 6 rows measures 10cm/4in over treble pattern using a 8mm (US L) crochet hook.

(Started at centre of bag base)
Make 26 chains.

Round 1: Work into 2nd chain, work 1 double crochet into each stitch to end, place marker, work 1 double crochet into remaining loop of each foundation chain to last chain, slip stitch to 1st double crochet to join. 50 stitches. Place marker at join.

Round 2: 1 chain (counts as 1 double crochet), 2 double crochet into next double crochet, 1 double crochet into each double crochet to 2 stitches before marker, 2 double crochet into next stitch, 1 double crochet into each of next 2 stitches, 2 double crochet into next stitch, 1 double crochet into each stitch to 2 stitches before end of round, 2 double crochet into next stitch, 1 double crochet into last stitch, join with a slip stitch to 1st chain. (4 increases)

Repeat round 2 5 times more. 74 stitches.

Place marker to show start of round which you will move as you work, and also another to remain in place to show side seam of bag.

Next round: 3 chain (counts as treble), miss first stitch, 1 treble into each treble to end, slip stitch to third chain at beginning of round to join.

Repeat this row until work measures 26cm/10in from beginning of section worked in trebles.

If necessary, turn and slip st into front of each stitch only back across to marker (you will then catch these slip stitches into work on following round), turn.

Next round: 1 chain, 1 double crochet into each stitch to end, slip stitch to first stitch to join.

Repeat this round twice more.

Next round: 1 chain, 1 double crochet into next 10 stitches, chain 17, miss next 17 stitches, 1 double crochet into next 20 stitches, chain 17, miss next 17 stitches, 1 double crochet into next 10 stitches, slip stitch to 1st stitch to join.

Next round: 1 chain, 1 double crochet into next 10 stitches, work 1 double crochet into next 17 chains, 1 double crochet into next 20 stitches, work 1 double crochet into next 17 chains, 1 double crochet into next 10 stitches, slip stitch to 1st stitch to join.

Next round: 1 chain, 1 double crochet into each stitch to end, slip stitch to first stitch to join.

Repeat this round 4 times more.

Fasten off and sew in ends. You may wish to line the bag with fabric.

SHRUG

ROWAN SOFTKNIT COTTON

FINISHED SIZE

S	M	L	XL	XXL
To fit UK dress size				
8-10	12-14	16-18	20-22	24-26

MATERIALS

YARN

Rowan Softknit Cotton
5 [5:7:7:7] x 50gm
Shown in Aged Rose 583

Also suitable for Rowan Handknit Cotton

HOOK

4mm (G6) crochet hook

TENSION

15 stitches and 10 rows measures 10cm/4in over pattern using a 4mm (G6) crochet hook.

Work 8 chains and join with a slip stitch to form a ring.

Round 1: 1 chain, work 12 double crochet into ring, slip stitch into first double crochet to join.

Round 2: 5 chain (counts as 1 treble and 2 chain), (1 treble into next stitch, work 2 chain) 11 times, slip stitch into 3rd chain at beginning of round to join.

Round 3: Slip stitch across into next chain space, 4 chain (counts as 1 treble and chain), * 1 treble into next chain space, 2 chain, (3 trebles, 2 chain, 3 trebles) into next chain space, 2 chain , 1 treble into next chain space, 1 chain, rep from * twice more, 1 treble in next chain space, 2 chain, (3 treble, 2 chain, 3 treble) into next chain space, 2 chain, slip stitch into 3rd chain at beginning of round.

Round 4: Slip stitch across into next chain space, 4 chain (counts as 1 treble and chain), * 1 treble into next chain space, 2 chain, (3 trebles, 2 chain, 3 trebles) into next chain space, 2 chain, (1 treble into next chain space, 1 chain) twice, rep from * twice more, 1 treble in next chain space, 2 chain, (3 treble, 2 chain, 3 treble) into next chain space, 2 chain, 1 treble into next chain space, 1 chain, slip stitch into 3rd chain at beginning of round.

Round 5: Slip stitch across into next chain space, 4 chain (counts as 1 treble and chain), * 1 treble into next chain space, 2 chain, (3 trebles, 2 chain, 3 trebles) into next chain space, 2 chain, (1 treble into next chain space, 1 chain) 3 times, rep from * twice more, 1 treble in next chain space, 2 chain, (3 treble, 2 chain, 3 treble) into next chain space, 2 chain, (1 treble into next chain space, 1 chain) twice, slip stitch into 3rd chain at beginning of round.

Round 6: Slip stitch across into next chain space, 4 chain (counts as 1 treble and chain), * 1 treble into next chain space, 2 chain, (3 trebles, 2 chain, 3 trebles) into next chain space, 2 chain, (1 treble into next chain space, 1 chain) 4 times, rep from * twice more, 1 treble in next chain space, 2 chain, (3 treble, 2 chain, 3 treble) into next chain space, 2 chain, (1 treble into next chain space, 1 chain) 3 times, slip stitch into 3rd chain at beginning of round.

Round 7: Slip stitch across into next chain space, 4 chain (counts as 1 treble and chain), * 1 treble into next chain space, 2 chain, (3 trebles, 2 chain, 3 trebles) into next chain space, 2 chain, (1 treble into next chain space, 1 chain) 5 times, rep from * twice more, 1 treble in next chain space, 2 chain, (3 treble, 2 chain, 3 treble) into next chain space, 2 chain, (1 treble into next chain space, 1 chain) 4 times, slip stitch into 3rd chain at beginning of round.

Round 8: Slip stitch across into next chain space, 4 chain (counts as 1 treble and chain), * 1 treble into next chain space, 2 chain, (3 trebles, 2 chain, 3 trebles) into next chain space, 2 chain, (1 treble into next chain space, 1 chain) 6 times, rep from * twice more, 1 treble in next chain space, 2 chain, (3 treble, 2 chain, 3 treble) into next chain space, 2 chain, (1 treble into next chain space, 1 chain) 5 times, slip stitch into 3rd chain at beginning of round.

Round 9: Slip stitch across into next chain space, 5 chain (counts as 1 treble and 2 chain), * 1 treble into next chain space, 2 chain, (3 trebles, 2 chain, 3 trebles) into next chain space, 2 chain, (1 treble into next chain space, 2 chain) 7 times, rep from * twice more, 1 treble in next chain space, 2 chain, (3 treble, 2 chain, 3 treble) into next chain space, 2 chain, (1 treble into next chain space, 2 chain) 6 times, slip stitch into 3rd chain at beginning of round.

Round 10: Slip stitch across into next chain space, 5 chain (counts as 1 treble and 2 chain), * 1 treble into next chain space, 2 chain, (3 trebles, 2 chain, 3 trebles) into next chain space, 2 chain, (1 treble into next chain space, 2 chain) 8 times, rep from * twice more, 1 treble in next chain space, 2 chain, (3 treble, 2 chain, 3 treble) into next chain space, 2 chain, (1 treble into next chain space, 2 chain) 7 times, slip stitch into 3rd chain at beginning of round.

Rounds 9 and 10 set pattern, continue in this way working an extra 1 treble, 2 chain on each side on every further round.

If you reach a point when your work starts to not lay flat on the next row add an extra chain to each chain space apart from the corner (3 treble, 2 chain, 3 treble into next chain space) which will remain the same throughout, not forgetting to add one to the chains at the beginning of the round.

For example – **Next round:** Slip stitch across into next chain space, 6 chain (counts as 1 treble and 3 chain), * 1 treble into next chain space, 3 chain, (3 trebles, 2 chain, 3 trebles) into next chain space, 3 chain space, (1 treble into next chain space, 3 chain) until 1 chain space remains before corner, rep from * twice more, 1 treble in next chain space, 3 chain, (3 treble, 2 chain, 3 treble) into next chain space, 3 chain, (1 treble into next chain space, 3 chain) to last chain space, slip stitch into 3rd chain at beginning of round.

Continue in this way until work measures approx. 58 [63:69:75:82] cm/23[25:27:29½:32½]in.

Next round: 1 chain, work double crochet around edge of work working 1 double crochet into each stitch and the same number into each chain space as there are chains, slip stitch to 1st double crochet to join.

Next round: 1 chain, work 1 double crochet into each stitch to end, working 1 chain at each corner to help your work lay flat, slip stitch to 1st double crochet to join.

Press your work. Fold square in half, then join 6 [6:7:7:8]cm/2½ [2½:3:3:3¼]in at the beginning of each short side either using a crochet slip stitch through both pieces of fabric or by sewing the seam.

CHEVRON SCARF

ROWAN SOFTKNIT COTTON

MATERIALS

YARN

Rowan Softknit Cotton
(shown in Aged Rose 583)

Also suitable for Rowan Handknit Cotton

1 ball will work approx. 56cm/22in of
18cm/7in wide scarf.

I made mine approx. 164cm/64½in long

HOOK

4mm (US G6) crochet hook

TENSION

Approx. 15 stitches and 10 rows over
pattern measures 10cm/4in using a 4mm
(US G6) crochet hook.

Make 39 chains.

Row 1: Work 1 treble into 4th chain from
hook, 1 treble into next 4 chains, * miss 2
chains, 1 treble into next 5 chains, work 2
chain, 1 treble into next 5 chains, repeat
from * once more, miss 2 chains, 1 treble
into next 4 chains, 2 trebles into last chain.

Row 2: Work 3 chain, 1 treble into stitch at
base of chain, * 1 treble into next 4 stitches,
miss 2 stitches, 1 treble into next 4 stitches,
(work 1 treble, 2 chain, 1 treble) into next
chain space, repeat from * once more, miss
2 stitches, 1 treble into next 4 stitches, 2
trebles into top of 3 chain at beginning of
previous row.

Row 2 sets pattern.

Continue in pattern as set until scarf
measures desired length.

Cut yarn and fasten off. Sew in any ends.

STRIPED SCARF

ROWAN HANDKNIT COTTON

FINISHED SIZE

12cm x 146cm/4½in x 57½in

MATERIALS

YARN

Rowan Handknit Cotton
A – Slate 347 3 x 50gm
B – Delphinium 334 1 x 50gm

Also suitable for Rowan Softknit Cotton

HOOK

4mm (US 6) crochet hook

TENSION

15 stitches and 10 rows measures 10cm/4in
over pattern using a 4mm (US 6) crochet
hook.

Using A make 222 chains.

Row 1: Using A, treble into 4th chain from
hook, treble into each stitch to end, turn.

Row 2: Chain 3, miss first treble, * 1 treble
into each stitch to end, ending with treble
into 3rd chain at end of last row, turn.

Row 3: Using B chain 1, * double crochet
into next 2 stitches, place hook into centre
of treble 1 row below next stitch, take yarn
over hook and pull through, take yarn over
hook and pull through these two loops, double crochet into next stitch, repeat from * to
last stitch, double crochet in to next stitch,
double crochet into 3rd chain at end of last
row, turn.

Row 4: Chain 1, double crochet into each
stitch to end of row.

These 4 rows set pattern.
Work 14 rows more in pattern as set, ending
with row 2.

Cut yarn and fasten off. Sew in ends.

The scarf can be made wider by working
more rows but make sure you end with row
2 of the pattern.

MATERIALS

YARN
Rowan Softknit Cotton or Handknit Cotton
Shorter version – approx. half a ball
Longer version – 1 x 50gm

Both versions shown in Softknit Cotton,
shorter version in Dark Lime 579, longer
version in Seaweed

Handmade ceramic button from
www.deehardwicke.co.uk

HOOK
4mm (US G6) crochet hook

NOTE
These patterns are written using UK crochet
abbreviations for US see information page.

FOR SHORTER VERSION

Make 80 chains.

Row 1: Work 1 double crochet in to 7th
chain from hook (this loop will form button-
hole), work 1 double crochet into each chain
to end. 73 stitches.

Measure around neck and if the necklace
feels too tight you will need to begin again
with more stitches but you will need to add a
multiple of 6 stitches in order for the pattern
to work correctly.

Row 2: 3 chain, miss 3 stitches, * work (3
treble, 3 chain, 3 treble) all into next stitch,
miss 2 stitches, 1 treble into next stitch, miss
2 stitches, repeat from * to last 6 stitches,
work (3 treble, 3 chain, 3 treble) all into next
stitch, miss 2 stitches, 1 treble into last stitch.

Row 3: 3 chain, miss 3 stitches, * work (3
treble, 4 chain, 3 treble) all into next stitch,

COLLAR
ROWAN SOFTKNIT COTTON

miss 2 stitches, 1 treble into next stitch, miss 2 stitches, repeat from * to last 6 stitches, work (3 treble, 4 chain, 3 treble) all into next stitch, miss 2 stitches, 1 treble into last stitch.

Row 4: 3 chain, miss 3 stitches, * work (3 treble, 4 chain, 3 treble) all into next stitch, 1 chain, miss 2 stitches, 1 treble into next stitch, 1 chain, miss 2 stitches, repeat from * to last 6 stitches, work (3 treble, 4 chain, 3 treble) all into next stitch, miss 2 stitches, 1 treble into last stitch.

Row 5: 1 chain,* 1 double crochet into each of next 3 stitches, (2 double crochet, chain 4, 2 double crochet) into chain space, 1 double crochet into each of next 3 stitches, * 1 double crochet into chain space, 1 double crochet into next stitch, 1 double crochet into chain space, (2 double crochet, chain 4, 2 double crochet) into chain space, 1 double crochet into each of next 3 stitches, repeat from * to end, work double crochet into 3rd chain at beginning of round.

Fasten off and sew in ends. Sew on button.

FOR LONGER VERSION

Work as given for short version to end of row 4.

Row 5: 3 chain, miss 3 stitches, * work (3 treble, 5 chain, 3 treble) all into next stitch, 1 chain, miss 2 stitches, 1 treble into next stitch, 1 chain, miss 2 stitches, repeat from * to last 6 stitches, work (3 treble, 5 chain, 3 treble) all into next stitch, miss 2 stitches, 1 treble into last stitch.

Row 6: 3 chain, miss 3 stitches, * work (3 treble, 5 chain, 3 treble) all into next stitch, 2 chain, miss 2 stitches, 1 treble into next stitch, 2 chain, miss 2 stitches, repeat from * to last 6 stitches, work (3 treble, 5 chain, 3 treble) all into next stitch, miss 2 stitches, 1 treble into last stitch.

Row 7: 1 chain,* 1 double crochet into each of next 3 stitches, (3 double crochet, chain 4, 3 double crochet) into chain space, 1 double crochet into each of next 3 stitches, * 2 double crochet into chain space, 1 double crochet into next stitch, 2 double crochet into chain space, (3 double crochet, chain 4, 3 double crochet) into chain space, 1 double crochet into each of next 3 stitches, repeat from * to end, work double crochet into 3rd chain at beginning of round.

Fasten off and sew in ends. Sew on button.

MESH COWL

ROWAN ALL SEASONS COTTON CHUNKY

FINISHED SIZE
68cm x 25cm/27in x 10in

MATERIALS

YARN
All Seasons Cotton Chunky
2 x 100gm
Shown in Powder 602

HOOK
10mm (US P) crochet hook

TENSION
9 stitches and 4.5 rows measures 10cm/4in
over pattern using a 10mm (US P) crochet
hook.

Make 62 chains, join with a slip stitch into
the 1ˢᵗ chain to form a ring.

Round 1: Make 1 chain, work 1 double
crochet into each chain to the end, slip
stitch to chain at beginning of round to join.

Round 2: Make 4 chains (this counts as the
first treble and first space), * miss 1 double
crochet, work 1 treble into next stitch, make
1 chain, repeat from * to end of round, slip
stitch to 3ʳᵈ chain at beginning of round to
join.

Round 3 − slipstitch into 1ˢᵗ chain space, 4
chain (counts as first treble and 1 chain), * 1
treble into next chain space, 1chain. Repeat
from * to end of round, slip stitch to 3ʳᵈ of
4 chain at the beginning of round to join.

Repeat round 3 until work measures
approx. 26cm/10in or desired height minus
1cm/½in.

Next round: Work as given for round 1.

Cut yarn and fasten off. Sew in ends.

The cowl can be made wider or narrower
by adding or subtracting stitches, but you
will need to keep an even number of
stitches to make the pattern work.

Step-by-Step

Techniques

MAKING A CHAIN

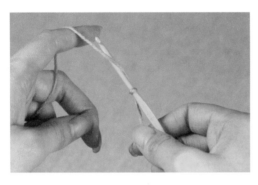

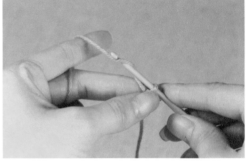

1: With a slip knot on the hook, take your yarn over the hook and twisting your hook to help, pull through the slip knot.

2: Take your yarn back over the needle and pull through the last chain formed as in step 1. Repeat step 2 until you have the correct number of chains (your slip knot will not count as a stitch).

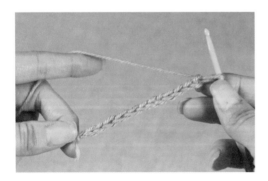

3: Try to keep the tension of your chain relaxed as if the stitches are too tight and small it will be hard to work into them.

DOUBLE CROCHET - on a foundation row

The instruction will tell you to leave some chain stitches at the beginning of the row, in order to create the height of the row of stitches.

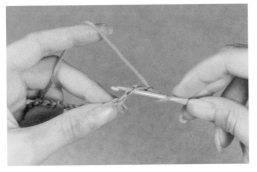 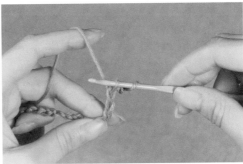

1: Working into the next stitch, place hook into the centre of the stitch making sure the hook is under 2 strands of the chain before using the hook to 'grab' the yarn.

2: Pull the yarn through the stitch, leaving two loops on the hook.

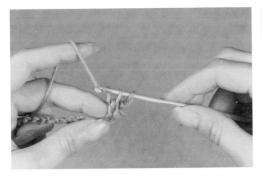 

3: Using your hook pull the yarn through both of these loops, leaving one loop remaining on the hook.

4 Once the stitch has been worked, continue in this way until all the stitches have been worked as set (following the pattern).

DOUBLE CROCHET - on already worked fabric

The instruction will tell you to work some chain stitches at the beginning of the row, in order to create the height of the row of stitches.

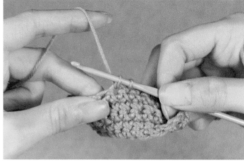

1: Working into the next stitch, place hook into the centre of the stitch before using the hook to 'grab' the yarn.

2: Pull the yarn through the stitch, leaving two loops on the hook.

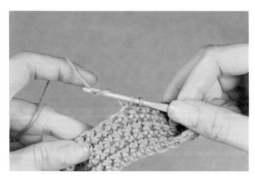

3: Using your hook pull the yarn through both of these loops, leaving one loop remaining on the hook.

4: Once the stitch has been worked, continue in this way until all the stitches have been worked as set (following the pattern).

TREBLE CROCHET - on a foundation row

The instructions will tell you to work some chain stitches at the beginning of the row, in order to create the height of the row of stitches.

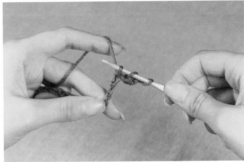

1: Take the yarn over the hook before placing the hook through the centre of the stitch to be worked , making sure the hook goes under the 2 top strands of the stitch.

2: Use the hook to grab the yarn and pull through the stitch, leaving three loops on the hook.

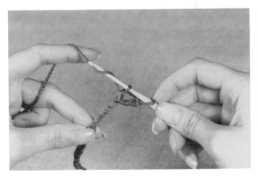

3: Using your hook grab the yarn and pull through the first two of these loops only, leaving two loops on the hook.

4: Using your hook grab the yarn and pull through the last two loops left on the hook, leaving one remaining.

TREBLE CROCHET - on already worked fabric

The instruction will tell you to work some chain stitches at the beginning of the row, in order to create the height of the row of stitches.

1: Take the yarn over the hook before placing the hook through the centre of the stitch to be worked.

2: Use the hook to grab the yarn and pull through the stitch, leaving three loops on the hook.

3: Using your hook grab the yarn and pull through the first two of these loops only, leaving two loops on the hook. Using your hook grab the yarn and pull through the last two loops left on the hook, leaving one remaining.

4: Once the stitch has been worked, continue in this way until all the stitches have been worked as set (following the pattern).

JOINING IN A NEW BALL OF YARN

1: On the last stitch worked using the old yarn work to the last step of the stitch so you have two loops on your hook.

2: Now complete your stitch ie using the hook to pull the new yarn through these two loops.

3: Sew in the ends of yarn.

SEWING IN ENDS

Some people choose to work in their ends as they crochet but here we will show you how to sew in your ends which is simpler for beginners.

1: Thread the yarn tail through a blunt ended sewing needle.

2: Feed the needle through the centre of the row of stitches either above or below for approx. 5cm/2in.

3: Bring your yarn to the back of your work, leaving half a stitch and then feeding it back through the stitches again before cutting the end. By wrapping the yarn around part of a stitch and feeding it back through you will create a more secure finish.

FINISHING YOUR WORK

1: When you have completed your work, with the last loop of the last stitch on your needle use your hook to enlarge the loop.

2: Cut your yarn leaving a tail approx. 10cm/4in in length and feed this tail through the centre of the enlarged loop.

3: Pull tail to tighten and this end can then be sewn in to your work.

If you are left handed it will help to hold the book up to a mirror and follow the reflection.

Information

UK vs US crochet abbreviations

In this book we have used UK crochet terms which differ slightly to the US terms. Whilst In this book we have given you a description of how each stitch is worked, we have included a couple of UK terms and the relative US terms for your future reference.

UK	US
Double crochet	Single crochet
Treble	Double crochet

Tension

This is the size of your crochet. Most of the patterns will have a tension quoted. This is how many stitches in width and how many rows in length It takes to make a 10cm/4in square. If your crochet doesn't match this then your finished garment will not measure the correct size. To obtain the correct measurements for your garment you must achieve the tension.

The tension quoted on a ball band is the manufacturer's average. For the manufacturer and designers to produce designs they have to use a tension for you to be able to obtain the measurements quoted. It's fine not to be the average, but you need to know if you meet the average or not. Then you can make the necessary adjustments to obtain the correct measurements.

How to make a Tension Square

First of all look at the tension details in your pattern. For example it might say "20 stitches and 28 rows to 10cm/4in measured over pattern using a 4mm crochet hook". Make sure you use the correct yarn and needles. Make your initial chain at least 4 extra stitches than the tension states (this will give you the true width of all stitches) and work at least 4 extra rows.

Your work might be looser or tighter than the tension required, in which case you just need to alter your hook size. Go up one size if you have an extra stitch or two sizes if you have two extra stitches and the reverse if you have fewer stitches.

Choosing Yarn

Choosing yarn, as one of my friends once described "It is like shopping in an adult's sweetie shop". I think this sums it up very well. All the colours and textures, where do you start? Look for the thickness, how chunky do you want your finished garment? Sometimes it's colour that draws you to a yarn or perhaps you have a pattern that requires a specific yarn. Check the washing/care instructions before you buy.

Yarn varies in thickness; there are various descriptions such as DK and 4ply these are examples of standard weights. There are a lot of yarns available that are not standard and it helps to read the ball band to see what the recommended hook size is. This will give you an idea of the approximate thickness. It is best to use the yarn recommended in the pattern.

Keep one ball band from each project so that you have a record of what you have used and most importantly how to care for your garment after it has been completed. Always remember to give the ball band with the garment if it is a gift.

The ball band normally provides you with the average tension and recommended hook sizes for the yarn, this may vary from what has been used in the pattern, always go with the pattern as the designer may change needles to obtain a certain look. The ball band also tells you the name of the yarn and what it is made of, the weight and approximate length of the ball of yarn along with the shade and dye lot numbers. This is important as dye lots can vary, you need to buy your yarn with matching dye lots.

YARN AMOUNTS ARE BASED ON AVERAGE REQUIREMENT AND ARE THEREFORE APPROXIMATE

Pressing and Aftercare.

Having spent so long knitting your project it can be a great shame not to look after it properly. Some yarns are suitable for pressing once you have finished to improve the look of the fabric. To find out this information you will need to look on the yarn ball band, where there will be washing and care symbols.

Once you have checked to see if your yarn is suitable to be pressed and the knitting is a smooth texture (stocking stitch for example), pin out and place a damp cloth onto the knitted pieces. Hold the steam iron (at the correct temperature) approximately 10cm/4in away from the fabric and steam. Keep the knitted pieces pinned in place until cool.

As a test it is a good idea to wash your tension square in the way you would expect to wash your garment.

Stockists

AUSTRALIA: Australian Country Spinners, Pty Ltd, Level 7, 409 St. Kilda Road,Melbourne Vic 3004. Tel: 03 9380 3888 Fax: 03 9820 0989 Email: customerservice@auspinners.com.au

AUSTRIA: Coats Harlander Ges.m.b.H.., Autokaderstraße 29, 1210 Wien, Austria Tel: 00800 26 27 28 00 Fax: (00) 49 7644 802-133 Email: coats.harlander@coats.com Web: www.coatscrafts.at

BELGIUM: Coats N.V., c/o Coats GmbH Kaiserstr.1 79341 Kenzingen Germany Tel: 0032 (0) 800 77 89 2 Fax: 00 49 7644 802 133 Email: sales.coatsninove@coats.com Web: www.coatscrafts.be

BULGARIA: Coats Bulgaria, 7 Magnaurska Shkola Str., BG-1784 Sofia, Bulgaria Tel: (+359 2) 976 77 41 Fax: (+359 2) 976 77 20 Email: officebg@coats.com Web: www.coatsbulgaria.bg

CANADA: Westminster Fibers, 10 Roybridge Gate, Suite 200, Vaughan, Ontario L4H 3M8 Tel: (800) 263-2354 Fax: 905-856-6184 Email: info@westminsterfibers.com

CHINA: Coats Shanghai Ltd, No 9 Building , Baosheng Road, Songjiang Industrial Zone, Shanghai. Tel: (86- 21) 13816681825 Fax: (86-21) 57743733-326 Email: victor.li@coats.com

CYPRUS: Coats Bulgaria, 7 Magnaurska Shkola Str., BG-1784 Sofia, Bulgaria Tel: (+359 2) 976 77 41 Fax: (+359 2) 976 77 20 Email: officebg@coats.com Web: www.coatscrafts.com.cy

CZECH REPUBLIC: Coats Czecho s.r.o.Staré Mesto 246 569 32Tel: (420) 461616633 Email: galanterie@coats.com

ESTONIA: Coats Eesti AS, Ampri tee 9/4, 74001 Viimsi HarjumaaTel: +372 630 6250 Fax: +372 630 6260 Email: info@coats.ee Web: www.coatscrafts.co.ee

DENMARK: Carl J. Permin A/S Egegaardsvej 28 DK-2610 Rødovre Tel: (45) 36 72 12 00 E-mail: permin@permin.dk

FINLAND: Coats Opti Crafts Oy, Huhtimontie 6 04200 KERAVA Tel: (358) 9 274871 Email: coatsopti.sales@coats.com www.coatscrafts.fi

FRANCE: Coats France, c/o Coats GmbH, Kaiserstr.1, 79341 Kenzingen, Germany Tel: (0) 0810 06 00 02 Email: artsdufil@coats.com Web: www.coatscrafts.fr

GERMANY: Coats GmbH, Kaiserstr. 1, 79341 Kenzingen, Germany Tel: 0049 7644 802 222 Email: kenzingen.vertrieb@coats.com Fax: 0049 7644 802 30 Web: www.coatsgmbh.de

GREECE: Coats Bulgaria, 7 Magnaurska Shkola Str., BG-1784 Sofia, Bulgaria Tel: (+359 2) 976 77 41 Fax: (+359 2) 976 77 20 Email: officebg@coats.com Web: www.coatscrafts.gr

HOLLAND: Coats B.V., c/o Coats GmbH, Kaiserstr.1, 79341 Kenzingen, Germany Tel: 0031 (0) 800 02 26 6488 Fax: 00 49 7644 802 133 Email: sales.coatsninove@coats.com Web: www.coatscrafts.be

HONG KONG: East Unity Company Ltd, Unit B2, 7/F., Block B, Kailey Industrial Centre, 12 Fung Yip Street, Chai Wan Tel: (852)2869 7110 Email: eastunityco@yahoo.com.hk

ICELAND: Storkurinn, Laugavegi 59, 101 Reykjavik Tel: (354) 551 8258 Email: storkurinn@simnet.is

ITALY: Coats Cucirini srl, Viale Sarca no 223, 20126 Milano Tel: 02636151 Fax: 0266111701

KOREA: Coats Korea Co. Ltd, 5F Eyeon B/D, 935-40 Bangbae-Dong, 137-060 Tel: (82) 2 521 6262 Fax: (82) 2 521 5181 Email: rozenpark@coats.com

LATVIA: Coats Latvija SIA, Mukusalas str. 41 b, Riga LV-1004 Tel: +371 67 625173 Fax: +371 67 892758 Email: info.latvia@coats.com Web: www.coatscrafts.lv

LEBANON: y.knot, Saifi Village, Mkhalissiya Street 162, BeirutTel: (961) 1 992211 Fax: (961) 1 315553 Email: y.knot@cyberia.net.lb

LITHUANIA & RUSSIA: Coats Lietuva UAB, A. Juozapaviciaus str. 6/2, LT-09310 Vilnius Tel: +370 527 30971 Fax: +370 527 2305 Email: info@coats.lt Web: www.coatscrafts.lt

LUXEMBOURG: Coats N.V., c/o Coats GmbH, Kaiserstr.1, 79341 Kenzingen, Germany Tel: 00 49 7644 802 222 Fax: 00 49 7644 802 133 Email: sales.coatsninove@coats.com Web: www.coatscrafts.be

MALTA: John Gregory Ltd, 8 Ta'Xbiex Sea Front, Msida MSD 1512, Malta Tel: +356 2133 0202 Fax: +356 2134 4745 Email: raygreg@onvol.net

MEXICO: Estambres Crochet SA de CV, Aaron Saenz 1891-7, PO Box SANTAMARIA, 64650 MONTERREY TEL +52 (81) 8335-3870

NEW ZEALAND: ACS New Zealand, P.O Box 76199, Northwood, Christchurch New Zealand Tel: 64 3 323 6665 Fax: 64 3 323 6660 Email: lynn@impactmg.co.nz

NORWAY: Falk Knappehuset AS, Svinesundsveien 347, 1788 Halden, Norway Tel: +47 555 393 00 Email: post@falkgruppen.no

PORTUGAL: Coats & Clark, Quinta de Cravel, Apartado 444, 4431-968 Portugal Tel: 00 351 223 770700

SINGAPORE: Golden Dragon Store, 101 Upper Cross Street #02-51, People's Park Centre, Singapore 058357 Tel: (65) 6 5358454 Fax: (65) 6 2216278 Email: gdscraft@hotmail.com

SLOVAKIA: Coats s.r.o.Kopcianska 94851 01 Bratislava Tel: (421) 263532314 Email: galanteria@coats.com

SOUTH AFRICA: Arthur Bales LTD, 62 4th Avenue, Linden 2195 Tel: (27) 11 888 2401 Fax: (27) 11 782 6137 Email: arthurb@new.co.za

SPAIN: Coats Fabra SAU, Avda Meridiana 350, pta 13, 08027 Barcelona Tel: (34) 932908400 Fax: 932908409 Email: atencion.clientes@coats.com

SWEDEN: Bröderna Falk Sybehör & Garn Engros, Stationsvägen 2, 516 31 Dalsjöfors Tel: (46) 40-6084002 Fax: 033-7207940 Email: kundtjanst@falk.se

SWITZERLAND: Coats Stroppel AG, Stroppelstrasse 20, 5417 Untersiggenthal, Switzerland Tel: 00800 2627 2800 Fax: 0049 7644 802 133 Email: coats.stroppel@coats.com Web: www.coatscrafts.ch

TAIWAN: Cactus Quality Co Ltd, 7FL-2, No. 140, Sec.2 Roosevelt Rd, Taipei, 10084 Taiwan, R.O.C. Tel: 00886-2-23656527 Fax: 886-2-23656503 Email: cqcl@ms17.hinet.net

THAILAND: Global Wide Trading, 10 Lad Prao Soi 88, Bangkok 10310 Tel: 00 662 933 9019 Fax: 00 662 933 9110 Email: global.wide@yahoo.com

U.S.A.: Westminster Fibers, 8 Shelter Drive, Greer, South Carolina, 29650 Tel: (800) 445-9276 Fax: 864-879-9432 Email: info@westminsterfibers.com

U.K: Rowan, Green Lane Mill, Holmfirth, West Yorkshire, England HD9 2DX Tel: +44 (0) 1484 681881 Fax: +44 (0) 1484 687920 Email: ccuk.sales@coats.com Web: www.knitrowan.com

Acknowledgements

Many thanks to everyone that made this
book possible.

To the hugely talented and generally delightful
India Hobson for the lovely photography.
www.indiahobson.co.uk

To the equally delightful Emma at Orchis for the
stunning flowers. www.orchisfloraldesign.co.uk

To friends and family for all their support, especially
my mum for all the crocheting she did!

To Erica Pask for her superior crochet knowledge
and Darren for making the book beautiful.

Finally to Kate Buller and David MacLeod at
Rowan for their continued support.